DIRT ROAD DESTINY

FROM HUMBLE BEGINNINGS TO RESILIENT LEADERSHIP

BY
WENDELL B. SUMTER

ISBN: 979-8-9946333-2-8

Published by Wendell B. Sumter, Consulting and Motivational Speaking

Columbia, South Carolina

Printed in the United States of America

DEDICATION:

"To the women who paved my dirt roads with prayer: My mother, Luella, and my grandmothers, Nana and Julia. You built my 'faith muscle' and taught me that no road is too dusty for God to walk. This book is the fruit of the seeds you planted, and the destiny you saw before I ever could."

PREFACE

I grew up in Hopkins, South Carolina—on dirt roads, surrounded by family, faith, and community. I was always a "church boy," and my earliest memories include watching my grandmother, Ms. Neal, worship with abandon. Sometimes she was the only one shouting in church, but her strong faith left a mark on me. From her, I inherited what I call my "faith muscle."

My journey with God began long before I fully understood it. From preaching to cats, dogs, and chickens on my grandmother's porch, to singing in talent shows and choirs, the seeds of ministry and leadership were planted early. But it wasn't always easy. There were trials, struggles, and moments when I doubted my worth. I've been told I wasn't "college material," yet God wrote a different story. He opened doors, lifted me when I fell, and gave me opportunities beyond my imagination.

For over 30 years, I've been blessed to serve as both pastor and educator. Since 1993, I've pastored Zion Mill Creek Baptist Church in Columbia, SC, watching the church family grow in faith, unity, and ministry. In education, I began in the classroom, teaching with the conviction that every child can learn. God later expanded my territory—allowing me to serve as assistant principal, principal, and now Assistant Superintendent of Human Resources for Chester County School District. Along the way, I've seen schools flourish, students rise, and staff find joy in their work.

God's grace has also carried me around the world—to places like Prague, Spain, Amsterdam, and India—where I've had the privilege of inspiring educators, leaders, and students from every walk of life. Yet, no matter where I've traveled, I've remained humbled by the simple truth that I am blessed to be a blessing.

I am a son, a father to my only daughter, Kristin, and a proud " Papa to my granddaughter Mariah. I am also a pastor, a leader, and, above all, a servant of Christ. My story is not perfect—it's filled with hills and valleys, trials and triumphs. But it is a story of God's faithfulness.

This book is my testimony and my offering. It is proof that no matter where you begin, no matter the setbacks or voices of doubt you face, your story is not over. With God, your story can always change for the better.

I pray that as you read these pages, you'll find encouragement, strength, and hope. And most of all, I pray you'll be reminded that the Author of life is still writing your story too.

— Wendell B. Sumter

CONTENTS

Wendell Bernard Sumter's life story is a powerful testament to God's faithfulness and the transformative power of faith, family, and education. Born on February 9, 1968, in the rural community of Hopkins, South Carolina, Wendell's childhood was shaped by the strong Christian faith and unwavering support of his grandmothers, Nana and Julia Dowdy. Nana's passionate worship and Julia's steadfast calm created a foundation of spiritual and familial grounding that would carry Wendell through the many trials and triumphs to come.

From an early age, Wendell displayed a natural gift for music, first discovering his singing voice at a family church anniversary. However, his desire to join the church choir led him to be baptized not out of a true understanding of salvation, but rather a childlike longing to use his talents. This imperfect beginning would foreshadow the way God would redeem Wendell's life, taking his flawed motives and turning them into a powerful ministry.

Wendell's journey took a challenging turn when he was wrongly placed in a special needs class in high school, only to be vindicated when his cousin advocated for him, and he tested out of the program. An even deeper blow came when a teacher crushed his spirit by declaring he was not "college material." Yet, Wendell refused to be defined by others' low expectations. He graduated from Morris College with a Bachelor's degree and went on to earn a Master's in Education, ultimately returning to his alma mater as the Assistant Principal—a poignant reversal that demonstrated God's redemptive hand.

College proved to be a season of both growth and struggle for Wendell. While he found brotherhood in Alpha Phi Alpha fraternity and spiritual community in the Baptist Student Union, he also wrestled with issues of identity, faith, and temptation. A supernatural encounter with a possessed individual deepened his understanding of spiritual warfare and his need to rely on God. It was during this time that Wendell made the pivotal decision to preach his first sermon, recognizing that God's call was greater than his own perceived shortcomings.

Tragedy struck when Wendell's mother, a survivor of both a heart attack and stroke, was diagnosed with cancer. Wendell's fervent prayers for her healing gave way to overwhelming grief and anger toward God when she ultimately passed away. Drawing strength from the biblical example of David's honest lament, Wendell learned to wrestle with his pain while also cultivating a spirit of gratitude, thanking God for the 70 years his mother lived and the years He allowed him to share with mother. This season of despair led him to a breaking point where he surrendered his burdens to God, discovering that true strength lies in trusting the Lord with what he cannot carry alone.

The COVID-19 pandemic presented Wendell with another challenge as he navigated the uncharted waters of pastoring without a physical congregation, preaching to empty pews while trusting that God's Word was not bound by walls. This experience reinforced the truth that not every battle belongs to him, but rather to the Lord—a lesson that would shape Wendell's approach to both ministry and life.

From the humble beginnings of preaching to animals on his grandmother's porch, Wendell's journey led him to the pulpit of Zion Mill Creek Baptist Church, where he has served as pastor since 1993. Under his leadership, the church has experienced remarkable growth, both numerically and spiritually, as Wendell has focused on cultivating a community of believers committed to making an impact rather than simply occupying seats.

Wendell's calling has extended beyond the church walls, as he has dedicated his career to education, viewing every classroom as a pulpit. Rising from teacher to principal, he has led schools to national recognition, all while practicing a servant leadership style that values people over position. Wendell's influence has even reached a global scale, as he has traveled the world training educators and inspiring students to reach their full potential.

Throughout his life, Wendell has navigated the delicate balance of ministry, fatherhood, and family. While he has faced the challenges of being a pastor and leader who is constantly in demand, he has learned that his first congregation is his own home. Wendell's relationship with his daughter, Kristin, and his granddaughter, Mariah, has become a cherished legacy, reminding him that true impact is measured not by the number of people in the pews, but by the depth of love poured into those closest to him.

As Wendell reflects on his life's journey, he recognizes that his story is not one of perfection, but of God's faithfulness in the midst of struggle. From being told he wasn't "college material" to traveling the world as an educator and ministry leader, Wendell's testimony is a testament to the transformative power of faith, the importance of mentorship and community, and the truth that every person's story matters. Wendell's life is a shining example of what's possible despite challenges that we all face.

CHAPTER 1

ROOTS IN HOPKINS

Hopkins, South Carolina, was nothing fancy—just dirt roads, wooden porches, and fields that stretched for miles. But it was there, on those dusty roads, that my destiny began. Hopkins was the kind of place most people would drive past without noticing. Back then, it was quiet and simple. We didn't have much by the world's standards, and yet never thought we were "poor." What we had was family, community, and faith—and that was more than enough.

Hopkins shaped me before I ever stepped onto a stage, into a pulpit, or in front of a classroom. Those early years gave me the foundation of everything I would one day become. I could ride my bike from home to my grandmother's house—whether it was Nana's or Grandma Julia's—and both places carried lessons that would stay with me for life.

Nana's Faith

My grandmother, Juliette D. Neal—"Nana"—was fire. She was a worshipper who didn't care if she was the only one shouting in church. If the Spirit moved her, she moved. I can still see her standing in the pew, rocking from side to side, hands lifted high, tears streaming down her cheeks.

As a boy, I sometimes felt embarrassed—why was she the only one shouting? But later, I realized she was teaching me that worship is personal. It's not about the crowd. It's not about what others think. Worship is about your connection to God.

Nana's faith wasn't just loud in church—it was strong in crisis. One day, she was babysitting some children. She stepped out to lock the gate, and somehow the car the children were sitting in slipped into gear. Nana tried to stop it, and the car rolled right over her leg.

I can still remember the chaos of that moment—the panic, the fear. She couldn't walk. But what do you do when life knocks you down? Nana called on prayer. She had people dial the prayer line, and we prayed as a family. After the prayer, Nana stood up and walked.

To this day, I can't explain it medically. Maybe the doctors missed something. Maybe there was another explanation. But I know what I saw: my grandmother walked on a leg that moments before couldn't hold her weight. God healed her. That miracle was my first real lesson that prayer changes things.

Grandma Julia's Calm

If Nana was the fire, then my other grandmother, Julia Sims Dowdy, was calm water. Where Nana would shout, Grandma Julia would quietly smile. Where Nana would raise her voice, Grandma Julia would speak softly. Some called her "Doll"—and I think it was because she was beautiful inside and out.

Her house became the center of our family life. Every Sunday after church, we piled into her home. The smell of collard greens, fried chicken, and cornbread filled the air. Cousins played outside, adults caught up in the kitchen, and the house buzzed with laughter.

But it wasn't just about Sunday dinners. Her house was our refuge. Whenever life got too heavy for my mom, whenever bills piled up, or struggles felt overwhelming, Grandma Julia's door was always open. She didn't need to preach sermons—her stability was her sermon.

I think every family needs that one person whose presence feels like peace. For us, that was Grandma Julia. She was the anchor that kept us steady.

Family Life and Work Ethic

Though my father, Herbert Neal, lived in Philadelphia, I was raised in Hopkins by my mother, Luella Sumter Dinkins, and my stepfather, Willie Dinkins Sr. But the truth is, I was raised by everybody. Family in Hopkins was like that—everybody had a hand in shaping your life.

I learned responsibility early. Believe it or not, one of my chores was feeding our hogs. And my step-granddaddy, Willie Dowdy Sr., farmed soybeans. My cousins and I would line up in those fields, pulling weeds for fifty cents a row. We thought we were working men then! Looking back, it wasn't about the money—it was about the lessons. Work hard. Do your part. And laugh while you're doing it.

Those days in the fields and around the hog pens may not sound glamorous, but they grounded me. They taught me the value of sweat, discipline, and family working side by side.

Childhood in Hopkins

Growing up in Hopkins wasn't glamorous, but it was rich in experience. We didn't have PlayStations or iPads, but we had dirt roads, imagination, and each other. We played kickball until the sun went down. We rode bikes down long, winding paths. We got dirty, scratched, and bruised, but those days built resilience in me.

I remember May Days at Hopkins Junior High School, when the community gathered for food, music, and games. I remember school talent shows, where kids like me tried to shine for just a few minutes on stage. I remember family reunions under the big oak tree—that oak still stands today—where cousins ran free, plates were full, and the spirit of togetherness filled the air.

Sometimes, we piled into cars and rode the bus to New Jersey for reunions, other times we stayed in South Carolina under the Big Oak Tree. Either way, I somehow always found myself strutting in front of the crowd like I was on a runway. Even then, God was preparing me to stand before people—though at the time I thought I was just showing off and being fashionable....LOL.

And of course, country life always had its surprises. I'll never forget the time I was out in my great-grandparents' pecan orchard and spotted a snake. Now, I like to say I was calm as a cucumber—but let me tell you, I took two or three long steps backward, then I took off running! I yelled for my uncle Herbert, who came running with his shotgun and shot the snake right there in the orchard. I laughed about that moment for years. Those were the kinds of memories that stitched Hopkins into my soul.

Discovering My Voice

It was in my grandmother's kitchen that I discovered my voice. One day, the Lydia Circle—my grandmother's church group—was preparing for an anniversary program. My cousin Tricia and I were asked to sing.

At first, I didn't think much of it. But when we stood in that kitchen and sang, the family's reaction shocked me. They clapped, shouted, and carried on like Luther Vandross and Diana Ross had just given a private concert. That moment planted confidence in me.

When I sang at the anniversary, the response from the crowd gave me a hunger for more. I realized I could move people with my voice, and something in me wanted to keep using it.

Baptized for the Wrong Reason

But here's the thing—back then, you couldn't sing in the choir unless you were baptized. Now, let me be honest—I didn't want baptism to be saved. I wanted baptism to sing!

So, I joined the church and was baptized—not even at my home church, but at my pastor's other church. I was so excited that I didn't even mind. My home church only baptized once a year after revival, but I couldn't wait that long. My motives weren't pure, but isn't it just like God to take our mixed-up reasons and use them anyway?

That baptism marked the official start of my walk with Christ. It didn't start perfectly, but it started. And sometimes, starting is all God asks for.

Reflection

When I look back on those Hopkins days, I see how God was already shaping me:

Nana's faith taught me prayer's power.

Grandma Julia's calm gave me stability.

Tricia and I singing awakened my gift.

Baptism for the choir began my walk with God—even if my reasons weren't right.

The dirt roads of Hopkins were more than childhood playgrounds. They were training grounds for destiny.

Key Scripture
*"Do not despise these small beginnings,
for the Lord rejoices to see the work begin."*
— Zechariah 4:10

Key Scripture
"But as for me and my household, we will serve the LORD."
— Joshua 24:15

1. Who in your family helped shape your faith?

2. What childhood experiences built resilience in you?

3. Have you ever started something for the "wrong" reason, but later saw God use it for His glory?

CHAPTER 2

FINDING MY VOICE

was just a boy from Hopkins, running dirt roads and trying to figure out life. But looking back now, I can see how God was already shaping me, giving me hints of what was to come. Music and preaching didn't show up in my life overnight. They started small, in the ordinary places where I least expected God to move.

May Day & Talent Shows

Hopkins Junior High was where I started stepping into myself. Back then, May Day was a big event. The whole school and community came together. There were games, food, music, and the big finale: the talent show.

By this point, I was in the 8th grade, and singing had become something I felt comfortable with. I had been in a school play that gave me even more confidence, and family reunions were always my stage to shine. Between those moments and May Day, I was starting to wonder if maybe my future would be in music or entertainment.

It's funny because in elementary school, when I was on the Mr. Kno zit show, I told everybody I wanted to be a fireman. Looking back now, maybe God still gave me that job—because as a leader, you're constantly putting out fires, just of a different kind! But by junior high, the stage felt like home, and I thought singing might just be my destiny.

When my cousin Theressa and I decided to enter the May Day talent show, we thought we had it made. We rehearsed, we practiced, we gave it our all. That night, when we stood on stage and sang "The Closer I Get to You" by Roberta Flack and Donny Hathaway, the crowd lit up. People stood to their feet, clapped, cheered, and pushed us higher with their energy. I just knew we had it.

But when the winners were announced, our names weren't called. Not first, not second, not even third. I was crushed. Devastated. All that excitement, all that support, and we still didn't place.

As I stood there disappointed, someone walked up to me and said, "You may not have won tonight, but there's greatness in you. You're going to be alright." That simple statement became fuel for me. It was as if God was whispering, "Your worth isn't measured in applause or trophies. I've got something bigger for you."

That hunger for the stage didn't stop there. Even when I went to Morris College years later, I entered the freshman talent show and sang my heart out. At the time, I still thought maybe singing was my calling. Little did I know, God was using those moments to train me—not just for songs, but for sermons.

Porch Preaching

While music was opening doors, something else was stirring, too. Back home on Granda's porch, I started my first "ministry." My congregation wasn't made up of people—it was cats, dogs, and chickens. I'd open a Bible, and preach like I'd heard pastors do on Sunday mornings.

The porch preaching was interesting because it didn't happen every day—it came in spurts. There were moments when I just felt a push, an urge from the Lord or the Spirit, to grab the Bible, go outside, and start reading scripture or giving a word. It didn't matter if my congregation had fur or feathers; what mattered was the joy I felt every time I opened my mouth.

It wasn't a strain. It wasn't something I forced. It felt natural, like it was what I was supposed to be doing. Even as a boy, it never felt negative or out of place. It felt like calling.

And that didn't stop on the porch. When I went to college, before I even formally accepted the call to preach, I found myself writing sermons. Sometimes, I'd even read those sermons or preach them to my roommates. Looking back, I see that those porch sermons were the beginning of my capacity to share the Word. God was shaping me, giving me boldness, and training me long before I ever stepped behind a pulpit.

The Anointing

A few weeks after the May Day disappointment, my grandmother took me to visit some cousins. It wasn't planned or anything special—we just went to their house like family often does. But God has a way of using ordinary moments to do extraordinary things.

The house was small, but they had a piano, and those women were spirit-filled. As we settled in, my grandmother did what grandmothers do—she started bragging: "My boy can sing." So they asked me to sing right there in their living room.

As I began to sing, something shifted. It wasn't just me singing a song—it felt like I was ministering. The room filled with jubilation and joy, and before I could finish, they had church right there. Then they did something I'll never forget: they brought out oil, placed their hands on my head, and began to pray over me.

The flow of the oil, the sound of their prayers, the atmosphere of that room—it was powerful, almost magical. I felt the anointing of the Holy Spirit in a way I never had before. It wasn't just emotion; it was presence. It was at that moment I began to realize that what God had placed in me could not remain dormant. Something had been stirred, awakened, and confirmed.

That day, I started to truly recognize what God had put inside of me.

Finding My Voice

Those experiences—the cheers of the crowd, the sting of losing, the porch preaching, and the anointing—became turning points. They taught me that voice isn't just about singing or speaking. Voice is about calling.

It's about how God takes ordinary kids on porches and in kitchens and whispers destiny into their ears. It's about how He uses disappointment to remind us that human applause isn't the goal—His purpose is. It's about how He takes small beginnings and turns them into lifelong callings.

That was when I started finding my voice—not just in music, but in ministry.

Key Scripture
"Before I formed you in the womb I knew you, before you were born I set you apart; I appointed you as a prophet to the nations."
— Jeremiah 1:5

FINDING MY VOICE: REFLECTION & ACTION

1. Can you remember a moment when someone spoke encouragement into your life at just the right time?

2. Have you ever felt overlooked or disappointed, but later realized God was using that moment to prepare you?

3. What "small beginnings" in your life might be God's way of training you for something greater?

CLOSING PRAYER

Lord, thank You for the people You send to speak encouragement into our lives. Help me to find my voice in You and to use it for Your glory. Remind me that even in disappointment, You are preparing me for destiny. Amen.

CHAPTER 3

MISPLACED AND MISJUDGED

Life has a way of putting labels on us. Sometimes people misplace us because they don't see our potential. Sometimes they misjudge us because of what they think we're capable of. I learned both lessons in high school, and they shaped the way I view education, leadership, and faith to this very day.

Misplaced in Special Ed

I'll never forget the day I walked into a special needs classroom. For reasons I didn't understand, I had been placed there. At first, I went along with it—sitting down, doing the work, wondering why I was there.

But my cousin, who was also in that class, wasn't having it. One day in the middle of class, he looked at the teacher and said, "He's not supposed to be in here. He's too smart for this."

The teacher raised an eyebrow. "Why do you say that?"

My cousin didn't back down. "Because I know him. Give him a test."

Finally, the teacher called me up to her desk, handed me a reading test, and told me to try. I sat down, nervous but determined, and worked through the assignment. When she graded it, she looked at me, then at my cousin, and said, "You're right. He doesn't belong in here."

Not long after, I was pulled from the special needs class and placed in a different track. On one hand, I was relieved. On the other hand, I carried the sting of being misplaced.

That experience stuck with me. It made me realize how easily students can be mislabeled, and how much it matters to have someone who will speak up for you. That moment with my cousin became a seed in my heart for the kind of educator and leader I would later become—someone who sees the potential in others, even when systems misplace them.

"You're Not College Material"

But being misplaced wasn't the end of it. Later, in a British Literature class, another blow came. One day, the teacher started talking with students about college. She looked at me and, with no hesitation, said:

"You're not college material."

Those four words crushed me. I can still feel the weight of them in my chest. My classmates turned and looked at me, and in that moment, I wanted to disappear. I felt embarrassed, exposed, and small. I walked out of that classroom with my spirit broken. In her eyes, I wasn't capable. I wasn't enough. I wasn't meant for higher education.

But isn't it just like God to take the very words meant to limit you and turn them into fuel?

I didn't just go to college—I graduated with a Bachelor of Science in Elementary Education from Morris College, where I became a proud, ice-cold brother of Alpha Phi Alpha Fraternity, Inc. I went further and earned my Master's Degree in Education from the University of South Carolina.

And God wasn't done. Years later, I walked back into my high school—not as a student, but as the Assistant Principal. The same teacher who once told me I wasn't college material now had to call me "Mr. Sumter."

That wasn't about revenge—it was about redemption. God had the final word.

Lessons from Misplacement & Misjudgment

Looking back, those two moments—being misplaced in special ed and being told I wasn't college material—were painful, but they shaped my calling. They taught me:

- Students need advocates. My cousin's voice mattered. Without him, I might have stayed mislabeled.

- Words matter. A teacher's comment almost broke me, but God's truth rebuilt me.

- Destiny is God's decision. No system, no test, no teacher has the authority to define your future. Only God does.

Ministry in Education

Those experiences also shaped my ministry as an educator. Every student who sat in my classrooms, every young person I mentored, I carried that memory with me. I asked myself, "Am I lifting this student up, or am I tearing them down? Am I seeing what God sees, or am I only judging what's in front of me?"

I remember one student in particular. He had been labeled a troublemaker, the kind of kid teachers whispered about in the lounge. But when I looked at him, I saw something different. Instead of focusing on his behavior, I started asking about his life, his dreams, and his challenges. Over time, he began to open up. By the end of that year, he wasn't just another "problem kid"—he was a leader among his peers.

That's when it hit me: the same way my cousin spoke up for me, I had the responsibility to speak up for students like him.

It's the same in church. Sometimes people come in broken, mislabeled, and misjudged. As pastors, leaders, and believers, we have to speak life over them, not death. We have to call out their potential, not their limitations.

I became an advocate because once upon a time, I needed one too.

Key Scripture
"The stone the builders rejected has become the cornerstone; the Lord has done this, and it is marvelous in our eyes."
— Psalm 118:22–23

MISPLACED AND MISJUDGED: REFLECTION & ACTION

1. Have you ever been mislabeled or misjudged by someone in authority? How did it affect you?

2. Who has spoken up for you as my cousin did for me—and how can you be that advocate for someone else?

3. Are there people in your life right now who need you to see their potential instead of their present?

CLOSING PRAYER

Father, thank You that my destiny is not determined by other people's opinions. Thank You that when the world misplaces or misjudges me, You still know exactly who I am. Help me to see others the way You see them, to speak life where others speak doubt, and to be an advocate for those who feel overlooked. Amen.

CHAPTER 4

THE COLLEGE YEARS

f high school was where I learned how cruel words could be, college was where I began to learn who I really was. Those years at Morris College were some of the best days of my life and some of the hardest. They were filled with laughter, brotherhood, struggles, doubts, faith, failures, and triumphs. College is where my calling began to take shape.

Finding My Place

When I first stepped on the campus of Morris College, I felt both excitement and fear. Here I was—the boy who was told he wasn't "college material"—walking onto a college campus with a chance to prove everyone wrong.

But it wasn't just about proving others wrong. It was about proving something to myself. Could I really do this? Could I rise to the challenge? At Morris, I discovered a community that pushed me. I found lifelong friendships, brotherhood, and a place where I could begin piecing together who I was.

Brotherhood in Alpha Phi Alpha

One of the most formative parts of my college experience was joining Alpha Phi Alpha Fraternity, Inc. Becoming a part of that brotherhood shaped me in ways I can't fully describe. It wasn't just about stepping, or wearing the letters, or the pride of being "ice cold." It was about discipline, accountability, and service.

Alpha Phi Alpha taught me what it meant to stand for something bigger than myself. It was a family that expected excellence, and it challenged me to rise to that level. The friendships I formed there are ones that still carry me today.

Testing Leadership: Running for SGA

College wasn't just about books, brotherhood, and worship for me. It was also where I started to test my leadership in bigger ways. I decided to run for Student Government Association President. I believed I could represent my classmates well, and I launched what I thought was a strong campaign.

I had posters, signs, and support across campus. My frat brothers stood with me, encouraging me, and I really thought I had a good shot at winning. I campaigned hard, spoke to students, and put my name out there with confidence.

But when the votes were counted, I lost—and not just by a little. My frat brothers, who were on the vote-counting committee, didn't even want to tell me how badly I lost. That was crushing. I had worked so hard, and it felt like another door slammed in my face.

But God always sends voices of encouragement at the right time. A little while later, I was in class with one of my professors, Dr. Bobby L. Brisbon, who was Chair of the Education Department. Out of the blue, he said to me, "I just want you to know—I felt like you were the best candidate. I don't know what happened, but from where I sit, you were the best."

That meant the world to me. His words reminded me that even in failure, my effort wasn't wasted. It reassured me that my leadership potential wasn't defined by one election. Losing didn't mean I wasn't a leader—it just meant God had other places for my leadership to grow.

The Baptist Student Union

Another part of my college journey was the Baptist Student Union (BSU). If Alpha Phi Alpha gave me discipline and pride, BSU gave me spiritual grounding. It was a place where I could worship, study, and be surrounded by other young people who were trying to live for God on a college campus.

That balance—fraternity on one side, BSU on the other—wasn't always easy. In fact, sometimes I struggled deeply with who I was. I was pulled between worlds: one that celebrated discipline, achievement, and social life, and another that demanded holiness, devotion, and sacrifice.

The Struggle

College was where I really began to wrestle with my identity. On one hand, I loved God. I read Scripture, I prayed, I even began preparing sermons. On the other hand, I struggled with sin. I went to parties, I worried about people's opinions, and I wrestled with insecurity and temptation.

There were nights I shouted and danced in church, and other nights I found myself in places I shouldn't have been. There were days I felt close to God and other days when I wondered if I'd ever measure up.

I share that honestly, because I know I'm not alone. Many of us have lived in that tension—loving God but struggling with sin, hearing the call but doubting our worthiness. I really felt like Paul in **Romans 7:21–25.** I find then a law, that, when I would do good, evil is present with me. For I delight in the law of God after the inward man: but I see another law in my members, warring against the law of my mind, and bringing me into captivity to the law of sin which is in my members. O wretched man that I am! Who shall deliver me from the body of this death? I thank God through Jesus Christ our Lord. So then, with the mind I myself serve the law of God; but with the flesh the law of sin.

Spiritual Warfare

One of the most unforgettable moments of my college years was when I encountered someone who was possessed or may have had a mental breakdown. He followed me several days on campus and believed that he was online for a fraternity. He even jumped into my car one night and refused to get out.. It shook me to my core. I wasn't prepared for it. I didn't know how to handle it. That night reminded me that spiritual warfare is real, and it isn't something to take lightly.

It pushed me deeper into prayer. It made me realize that being a Christian isn't just about going to church or reading the Bible. It's about living with the awareness that we are in a battle—not against flesh and blood, but against spiritual forces.

The Choice to Preach

It was during college that I made the decision to preach my first sermon. I had wrestled with the call for years. I had played church on Grandma's porch, I had been prayed over and anointed, but in college, it became real.

I still remember the nerves, the fear, the questions. "God, are You sure You mean me? I'm not good enough. I'm not holy enough. I'm not ready." But God doesn't call the qualified. He qualifies the called.

When I stood to preach for the first time, it wasn't polished. It wasn't perfect. The church was packed; it was standing room only. My sermon was on "Friends." In that moment, I knew: this was what God had been preparing me for all along.

Lessons from College

- Identity is found in God, not in approval.

- Brotherhood and community matter. We need people who push us higher.

- Struggle doesn't disqualify you. God uses imperfect people for His perfect plan.

- The call of God will find you—even in your mess.

Key Scripture
"Brothers and sisters, think of what you were when you were called. Not many of you were wise by human standards; not many were influential; not many were of noble birth. But God chose the foolish things of the world to shame the wise."
— *1 Corinthians 1:26–27*

THE COLLEGE YEARS: REFLECTION & ACTION

1. What was the biggest struggle you faced in your young adult years, and how did God use it to shape you?

2. Who in your life has given you the gift of brotherhood, sisterhood, or community?

3. Have you wrestled with the call of God? What steps might He be asking you to take right now?

CLOSING PRAYER

Lord, thank You for calling me even when I wasn't perfect. Thank You that my past struggles don't disqualify me from Your future plans. Help me to live boldly in my calling and to trust that if You called me, You will equip me. Amen.

CHAPTER 5

A MOTHER'S STRENGTH

My mother, Luella Sumter Dinkins, was a no-nonsense woman. She said what she meant and meant what she said. She didn't take junk from anybody. She was strong, outspoken, and deeply rooted in family. My grandmother used to say, 'That woman worships the ground you walk on.' And I believe she was right. My mom loved me unconditionally. She had a way of making me feel like I was her favorite—even though she loved all of her children.

Family First

She loved family gatherings. She was one of the organizers of our family reunions and made sure everyone stayed connected. When my grandmother Julia passed, Sunday dinners shifted to my mother's house. Her home became the hub of family life—the place where laughter, love, and food brought us all together.

Church Involvement

My mother was also an anchor in the church. She sang with the Jubilee Choir, chaired the food committee, and organized the pastor's pulpit aid ministry. When I became a pastor, she was my number-one supporter. She fought battles in the background that I couldn't fight publicly. She made sure I had someone standing with me, even when ministry was hard.

One of the things she always told me still rings in my ears today: 'Make sure you're real.' She didn't want me to play with God. She wanted me to walk in authenticity, to be true in my calling. That advice has shaped my ministry for decades.

The Battle with Cancer

My mom was a fighter. She beat cancer once, and we rejoiced. When it came back a second time, she endured chemotherapy and treatment like a champion. The third time was harder. The doctors suggested a major surgery, but she didn't want to go through it. Like many older people, she feared that if doctors cut on her,' the cancer would spread.

I'll never forget the day we came back from the doctor, and she sat me down to talk about her funeral wishes. It was sobering, but it showed her courage. She wasn't afraid to face reality.

A Christmas Memory

One of my fondest memories is of her love for Christmas. If she could have put Christmas lights on every blade of grass, she would have. Decorating her house and tree each year was my joy, because I knew it brought her so much happiness. That last Christmas with her is one I will never forget. I will never forget how she wanted me and my siblings to put up all of her decorations.I mean all of them, every tree, every light it was as if she knew this would be her last Christmas with us. We did just that, and it was a beautiful Christmas, not just because of the decor, but because we were all there and enjoyed our time with her. My aunts and uncles, the grandkids, cousins, everyone. It was a great Christmas.

Her Passing

Losing her was one of the hardest seasons of my life. When she died, it felt like the family lost its heartbeat. When my grandmother Julia passed, my mom became the mother to everyone in the family. When she was gone, it felt like a piece of us was missing.

Wrestling with God

When my mother passed, I didn't just grieve—I wrestled. I had prayed. Our family had prayed. We had asked God for healing. And I'll be honest—when it didn't come, I struggled with God.

Not long after her funeral, I went to a church service where someone gave a testimony about how God had healed their mother of cancer. How she had dried up to nothing and God turned things around and healed her, and while I clapped on the outside, on the inside I was angry. I thought, 'God, why her and not my mom? Didn't we believe? Didn't we pray?'

In my pain, I questioned God. I felt like He hadn't answered me. But then, not long after, a young woman in my church passed away. She was much younger than my mom. And in that moment, God reminded me: 'I am in control. I gave you 70 years with your mother—be grateful.'

It broke me. It humbled me. It shifted me from anger to gratitude. I realized that while she didn't get the healing I prayed for, I did get the blessing of time. Seventy years of her love, wisdom, laughter, and strength. And that was a gift I could never take for granted.

Lessons from My Mother

- Real love is unconditional.
- Strength is often quiet, fought behind the scenes.
- Authenticity in faith and leadership is non-negotiable.
- Even in sickness and suffering, faith can shine.

She also left me with sayings I still live by: 'Everybody ain't your friend.' 'A dog that carries a bone will bring a bone back.' And her constant reminder: 'Make sure you're real.' These weren't just words—they were life lessons.

Key Scripture
*"Her children arise and call her blessed; her husband also,
and he praises her: 'Many women do noble things,
but you surpass them all.'*
— Proverbs 31:28–29

A MOTHER'S STRENGTH: REFLECTION & ACTION

1. Have you ever wrestled with God when He didn't answer your prayers the way you expected?

2. How has God shifted your perspective from despair to gratitude in a difficult season?

3. What lessons or sayings from your parents or grandparents still shape you today?

CLOSING PRAYER

Lord, thank You for the gift of my mother's life. Thank You for her strength, her wisdom, and her unconditional love. Help me to carry her lessons forward with integrity. When I wrestle with disappointment, remind me that You are in control. May her legacy live on in the way I serve You, love others, and walk in authenticity. Amen.

CHAPTER 6

WHEN I COULDN'T CARRY IT ANYMORE

There comes a point in life when the weight gets too heavy. When you've done all you can do, prayed all you can pray, tried all you can try, and you still find yourself at the end of your strength. That's where I was.

Exhaustion

After my mom's diagnosis, after hospital visits, after trying to be strong for my family, the exhaustion finally hit me. I was worn out in my spirit, my body, and my emotions.

I remember coming home late from the hospital one night. Everyone else was asleep. The house was quiet, but inside of me, there was chaos. I sat in the dark living room with my tie loosened and my Bible still in my hand. The same Bible I had been reading at her bedside now lay heavy across my lap.

People looked to me for encouragement, for leadership, for faith. But what do you do when the encourager needs encouragement? What do you do when the one holding everyone else up feels like collapsing?

That was me. I was tired of smiling when I wanted to cry. Tired of preaching faith while secretly doubting. Tired of trying to fix something I couldn't fix.

The Breaking Point

One night, it all came to a head. I fell to my knees in that dark room and cried out to God:

"I can't do this anymore. I can't carry this. I can't try to fix this any longer. Here, God—take it. Please… carry it for me."

It wasn't a fancy prayer. It wasn't polished or poetic. It was raw, broken, and desperate. And that was exactly the prayer God was waiting for.

The Shift

In that moment, something changed. My circumstances didn't change right away—my mom was still sick, my problems were still real. But the weight lifted. I felt peace. I felt a release. I realized I had been carrying something that was never mine to carry.

God never asked me to be the savior. He just asked me to trust the Savior.

When I let go, I discovered that surrender isn't weakness—it's strength. Surrender isn't giving up—it's giving in to God's will.

Leadership Under Pressure

What I learned that night didn't just stay in my personal life. It reshaped me as a leader.

As a pastor, I had spent years thinking I had to fix everybody's problems—if someone was hurting, it was my job to heal them; if the church was struggling, it was my job to fix it; if a family was breaking apart, it was my job to put it back together.

And in education, the same weight was there. I was the administrator who carried the complaints of parents, the needs of teachers, and the struggles of students. I thought I had to hold it all together.

But when I broke that night, God reminded me: *You are not Me. Stop trying to be Me.*

I learned that leaders are not called to be superheroes. Leaders are called to point people to the real Savior. Recently, something funny happened. It was Christmas Day 2025, and I went by my daughter's house to drop off their Christmas gifts. As I brought the gifts into the house, my Mariah opened hers and said PaPa you're a savior, and I had to remind her, no Jesus is the SAVIOR. I knew what she meant, but wanted to make sure she knew who the real savior is.

A Pastoral Lesson

Not long after that moment of surrender, I preached a sermon that was unlike any I had preached before. Normally, I came to the pulpit polished, prepared, strong. But that Sunday, I was honest. I admitted that I was tired. I admitted that I had cried. I admitted that sometimes I didn't have all the answers.

And to my surprise, people responded more deeply than they ever had before. Tears flowed, not because I gave them three points and a poem, but because I was real.

That day I realized: people don't always need a perfect leader. Sometimes they need a human leader who can show them what trusting God really looks like.

The Freedom of Surrender

From that day forward, I made a choice: whenever I felt myself picking up burdens that weren't mine, I'd stop and pray, "Lord, this is Yours. I can't carry it, but You can."

I won't pretend it was easy. Sometimes I'd pick the burden back up without even realizing it. Sometimes I'd start worrying again about my mom, the church, the school, my family. But each time I remembered to lay it back at God's feet, peace would return.

That breaking point became a turning point.

From that breaking point, I discovered something that has guided me ever since: my **Balanced Life Plan (BLP).** These aren't just nice sayings. They're lessons I learned the hard way—through tears, through wrestling, through surrender. They became the principles that helped me keep walking when I thought I couldn't carry it anymore.

The Balanced Life Plan (BLP)

1. **Don't waste time worrying about things you can't control.**

   When my mom was fighting cancer, I wanted so badly to fix it. I researched treatments, prayed prayers, tried to stay strong. But no matter what I did, I couldn't control the outcome.

   Worry robbed me of peace until God reminded me: "This isn't yours to carry."

   Worry is a thief. It steals today's joy without changing tomorrow's outcome. The moment I stopped obsessing over what I couldn't control and placed it in God's hands, peace returned.

2. **You can't fight every battle. Choose which ones are worth fighting and let the others go.**

   As a pastor and leader, I learned this quickly. Not every rumor needs a response. Not every disagreement needs a war. Some battles are distractions meant to wear you down.

   When my mom was sick, I couldn't waste energy on petty arguments. My fight was for her, for my faith, and for my family's strength. I had to let go of the rest.

   Wisdom is knowing which battles belong to you—and which belong to God.

3. **When deciding on a work/life partner, think about whether this is the person you want to grow old with, not just someone who satisfies you now.**

   Life has taught me that partnership is not just about today's excitement but tomorrow's commitment. My mom modeled that kind of love—loyalty, strength, standing by family through storms.

   In leadership, in marriage, and in ministry, the real question is: Will this person stand with me in the storm?

4. **Surround yourself with good people. Goodness is contagious.**

   I thank God for my family, my fraternity brothers, my church family, and the mentors who spoke life into me. When I was misplaced in special ed, it was my cousin who spoke up. When I ran for SGA president in college and lost, it was Professor Brisbane who reassured me of my worth.

   The right people push you higher when you're ready to give up. The wrong people drain you. Choose wisely.

5. **Don't love only from your heart. Love from your head also.**

   Love is more than emotion—it requires wisdom. My mom used to say, "Everybody ain't your friend." That wasn't bitterness, it was wisdom.

   If you love only with your heart, you can get hurt. If you love with your head as well, you protect yourself while still giving the best of yourself. Love is a choice, not just a feeling.

6. **Live life to the fullest. Tomorrow is not promised to anyone.**

   Losing my mom reminded me of this truth. She loved life, especially Christmas lights. If she could have put lights on a blade of grass, she would have. She found joy in the little things.

Her example taught me: don't wait for perfect circumstances to celebrate. Don't keep putting off joy. Life is fragile, but joy is available today.

7. **It takes more muscles to frown than it takes to smile.**

Even in the darkest moments, laughter has healing power. Growing up on dirt roads, we didn't always have much, but we had joy. We laughed, played, and found ways to smile through the struggle.

In ministry, I've had to smile through pain, smile through loss, smile when I didn't feel like it. And you know what? That smile wasn't fake—it was faith. Smiling is a declaration that trouble won't have the last word.

Lessons from Surrender & Balance

- You can't carry what only God can handle.

- Surrender isn't failure—it's faith.

- Balance doesn't just happen. You choose it daily.

- People are helped more by your authenticity than your perfection.

Key Scripture
*"Come to me, all you who are weary and burdened,
and I will give you rest."*
— Matthew 11:28

WHEN I COULDN'T CARRY IT ANYMORE: REFLECTION & ACTION

1. What burden have you been carrying that God never asked you to carry?

2. Which battles are worth fighting—and which ones must you leave to God?

3. Who are the good people lifting you higher in this season?

4. Have you ever seen God use your brokenness to bless someone else?

5. What would it look like to live life to the fullest today?

———————— CLOSING PRAYER ————————

Lord, I confess I've tried to carry things I was never meant to carry. I give them to You right now. Take the weight, take the worry, take the pain. Give me Your peace in exchange for my burden. Teach me to trust You with what I cannot control. Help me live a life of balance, joy, and surrender. Amen.

CHAPTER 7

THE BATTLE BELONGS TO THE LORD

Life has a way of throwing battles at us that we never asked for. Some we can fight. Some we can't. Some require us to stand, others require us to kneel. And then there are battles that don't belong to us at all—they belong to the Lord.

The pandemic reminded me of that truth.

Uncertainty

Like everyone else, my world shifted when the pandemic hit. Suddenly, everything was uncertain. Doctor appointments felt scarier. Every day interactions felt dangerous. Plans were canceled, and the things we once took for granted—like worshipping in church together—were put on pause.

It wasn't just about sickness. It was about fear. Fear of the unknown. Fear of what was coming next. Fear of how long it would last.

I tried to keep encouraging others, but deep down, I wrestled with my own questions: *"God, what is happening? Where are You in all of this?"*

Preaching to Empty Pews

One of the hardest parts of that season was pastoring without people in the building. I'll never forget the first Sunday I walked into Zion Mill Creek, looked out from the pulpit, and saw nothing but empty pews.

No choir behind me. No congregation in front of me. No ushers at the door. Just me, a camera, and God.

I thought to myself, *"Lord, am I really preaching to empty seats? Does this even matter?"*

But as soon as I opened my mouth, the Holy Spirit reminded me that His Word is never bound by walls. Even though the sanctuary was empty, the Spirit was still full. The Word was still going forth—through livestreams, phones, and computer screens.

That season taught me that **the audience isn't the measure of the anointing.** God can move through one person listening on a cell phone just as powerfully as He can through a packed house. My job was to preach, whether to a crowd or a camera. The battle of encouragement, connection, and perseverance wasn't mine—it belonged to the Lord.

Not Every Fight Is Yours

That was when the Lord made it clear: not every fight is mine to fight. As Christians, we're called to be strong, but we're not called to be superheroes. Some battles belong to the Lord.

I thought about **King Jehoshaphat** in 2 Chronicles 20. When the armies came against him, he didn't draw his sword. He prayed. And God told him, *"The battle is not yours, but God's."*

That word came alive for me. I realized I was exhausting myself trying to fight battles I couldn't win—worrying about tomorrow, stressing about things out of my control, trying to be in charge of what only God could handle.

God's Faithfulness

As I surrendered those battles to Him, I started to see His faithfulness. God began moving in ways I never could. He opened doors, sustained me through challenges, and showed me that even in chaos, He is still in control.

The Lord gave His people hope. Every day, He gave just enough light for the step ahead. And somehow, in the middle of uncertainty, He restored peace to my heart.

Lessons from the Battle

Here's what I learned in that season:

Not every fight is your fight. Some battles are meant for God alone.

The anointing isn't measured by an audience. Even when pews are empty, God fills the room.

Prayer is more powerful than panic. When you stop stressing and start surrendering, peace follows.

God is faithful. Even in a global crisis, He remains the same yesterday, today, and forever.

Key Scripture
"Do not be afraid or discouraged because of this vast army. For the battle is not yours, but God's."
— 2 Chronicles 20:15

THE BATTLE BELONGS TO THE LORD: REFLECTION & ACTION

1. Have you ever felt like what you were doing didn't matter because no one was watching? How does knowing God sees you change that?

2. What battles are you trying to fight right now that you need to hand over to God?

3. How can prayer replace panic in your life?

CLOSING PRAYER

Lord, thank You that I don't have to fight every battle. Thank You that the battles too big for me belong to You. Help me to trust You when I don't understand, to rest when I want to worry, and to preach, pray, or lead even when it feels like no one is listening—because I know You are. Amen.

CHAPTER 8

FROM THE PORCH TO THE PULPIT

When I stood on my grandmother's porch as a little boy preaching to cats, dogs, and chickens, I had no idea where God was taking me. But every sermon to that "animal congregation" was preparing me. Every song I sang in the kitchen with Tricia was training me. Every anointing, every prayer, every tear, every "yes, Lord" whispered in private was leading to this: the call to preach the gospel.

Ordained to Preach

In 1990, I was ordained at **Zion Benevolent Baptist Church.** That moment was the official recognition of what God had already placed inside me. I had been preaching informally for years, but that day felt like a confirmation—a stamp of approval that said, *"Yes, God has called you. Now go and do the work."*

At Zion Benevolent, I served as Associate Pastor and wore many hats. I preached, taught, encouraged, and even directed the **C. L. Jackson Singers.** That choir had a sound, an energy, a spirit that filled the house. Music and preaching came together in powerful ways, and I was right in the middle of it.

But God wasn't going to let me stay comfortable for long.

Called to Pastor

In 1993, God called me to serve as Pastor of **Zion Mill Creek Baptist Church.** When I first stepped into that pulpit, I knew the Lord was up to something. Mill Creek wasn't just another assignment—it was family. It was purpose.

And let me tell you—**97 Mill Creek Parkway has been jumping ever since.**

At "The Creek," we didn't just have church, we lived it. We talked to our neighbors every Sunday, shared impromptu sermons, sang songs that came straight from the pulpit—sometimes remixed, sometimes brand new, but always from the heart.

We learned how to "Stand Still" while "Holding On in a Bad Place," how to praise with "No Shame in Our Praise," how to expect "Better," and how to look forward to "Overflow." Every Sunday was a reminder that God was still moving.

Growth and Miracles

Under God's guidance, Zion Mill Creek grew—not just in numbers, but in spirit. Membership expanded, ministries multiplied, property was acquired, and countless testimonies poured in. Lives were rededicated to Christ. Men and women accepted their calls into ministry. The church became more than a building—it became a family.

One of the greatest joys has been watching people discover that church isn't about position or title, it's about contribution. That's been my focus since day one: not the seat you sit in, but the impact you make.

Ministry in the Pandemic

When the pandemic hit, "The Creek" faced a challenge like never before. For a season, there were no packed pews, no choir filling the air with song, no ushers greeting at the door. Just cameras, microphones, and a preacher determined to keep the Word alive.

But what could have silenced us actually stretched us. We learned to livestream, to worship in our living rooms, to fellowship through phone calls and Zoom screens. We discovered that the church is not confined to four walls.

And when we finally returned to in-person worship, we came back stronger. There was a new fire, a deeper gratitude, a greater unity. We had been through the storm, and God brought us through.

The Heart of a Pastor

Being a pastor isn't glamorous. It's not about robes, titles, or recognition. It's about walking with people through their highest highs and lowest lows. It's about funerals and weddings, hospital visits, and baby dedications, counseling sessions, and altar calls.

It's about being interrupted in the grocery store for prayer. It's about receiving phone calls at midnight. It's about loving people even when they don't always love you back.

But if I had to choose again, I'd still say yes. Because there is no greater joy than watching lives change, families restored, and souls saved.

Lessons from the Pulpit

From porch to pulpit, I've learned:

Calling grows in stages. God often starts small before He takes you big.

Church is about contribution, not position. Titles fade, but impact lasts.

Obedience is the key to overflow. Say yes to God, and He'll do more than you can imagine.

Even empty pews can't silence God's Word.

Key Scripture
"I will give you shepherds after my own heart, who will lead you with knowledge and understanding."
— Jeremiah 3:15

1. Who in your life has been a spiritual shepherd to you, guiding you closer to God?

2. In what ways are you contributing to your church family beyond just attending?

3. How has God used seasons of challenge (like the pandemic) to grow your faith and your church?

CLOSING PRAYER

Lord, thank You for calling me from porch to pulpit. Thank You for trusting me to shepherd Your people. Help me to serve with humility, to lead with love, and to never forget that the church is not about buildings or titles—it's about You. Amen.

CHAPTER 9

EDUCATOR AT HEART

God didn't just call me to preach in the pulpit. He also called me to teach in the classroom. My heart has always been for people, and for much of my life, that heart has beat strongest for students. Education has been one of the greatest ministries God has given me. It all started with Aunt Dianne. My biggest inspiration to become an educator came from my aunt, Dianne Singleton. She was a teacher for many years, and during the summers when I was a little boy, she would take me with her to her school to help prepare her classroom for the new year. For most kids, summer meant sleeping late, playing outside, or going to the pool. But for me, the highlight of summer was going with Aunt Dianne to set up her classroom.

The moment we walked through the doors of that school, I felt like I was stepping into a world of possibilities. I wasn't just a little boy tagging along—I felt like I belonged there. She would give me small tasks, but to me, they were significant responsibilities. I arranged desks, making sure each one was perfectly aligned. I tacked colorful borders on bulletin boards with the precision of a professional decorator. I organized the bookshelf, so every story had its place. And my favorite part of all—placing the name cards on each student's desk.

It wasn't my classroom, but in my heart, it felt like it was. I could almost picture the students who would come in on the first day, sitting down at those desks, ready to learn. It gave me joy to know I was helping create a space where children would grow, laugh, and dream.

Those summers did more than give me something to do—they gave me vision. They planted a seed in me that never went away. Even when I was misplaced in a special education class, even when a teacher told me I wasn't "college material," there was still something in me that longed to teach, to lead, to make a difference in the lives of students.

Looking back now, I see how God used those simple summer days to whisper destiny into my spirit. While I thought I was just helping my aunt, God was showing me the first glimpses of my own calling. Aunt Dianne didn't just let me help in her classroom—she helped me prepare for mine.

The Classroom as a Pulpit

When I began teaching, I quickly realized that the classroom was its own kind of sanctuary. Every morning, I stood before a congregation of students. Instead of pews, there were desks. Instead of a choir, there was the hum of chatter before the bell rang.

And instead of preaching sermons, I taught lessons. Math problems, reading assignments, and history projects. But woven through every subject was a more profound message: *"You matter. You can succeed. You are capable."*

I understood the power of a teacher's words because I had lived through words that wounded me. I had heard *"You're not college material."* And I had proved those words wrong. I carried that memory into every classroom I entered.

So, when I stood before students, I wasn't just teaching—I was pastoring. I was speaking life into young people who didn't always hear it anywhere else.

Leadership in Education

After years of teaching at the elementary and middle school levels, God opened new doors. I returned to my alma mater, Lower Richland High School, not as a student but as the Assistant Principal.

Walking those halls as a leader was surreal. I had once been just another student in those classrooms, struggling with insecurity and identity. Now, I was helping shape the culture of the school, guiding teachers, and leading students toward excellence.

From there, I went on to serve as Principal of Great Falls Middle School and Great Falls Elementary School. That season stretched me, challenged me, and grew me as a leader. It was there I learned that leadership is not about power—it's about service.

Servant Leadership & GTTM

I tried to lead the way Jesus led: as a servant. That meant doing things people didn't always expect a principal to do.

One time, I cooked steak dinners to show appreciation for my faculty and staff. Another time, I kissed a pig to motivate my students. (Yes, you read that right—I kissed a pig!)

That pig-kissing moment wasn't just a stunt—it was a **celebration of achievement.** I had promised my students that if they outperformed the district, I'd do it. When the scores came in, and they had outscored every other school, I kept my word. The students roared with laughter, the teachers clapped, and that silly act sent a serious message:

"I believe in you. Your hard work matters. And I'll do whatever it takes to celebrate your success."

That's when I realized I had stumbled onto another principle of leadership that I carry with me to this day: **GTTM — Give Them the Motivation.**

Motivation doesn't always come from lectures or rules. Sometimes it comes from creativity, humor, or even humility. Students — and adults — need to see leaders who are willing to put skin in the game, to risk looking silly, to inspire them to push harder.

One of my teachers once told me, *"Mr. Sumter, you could sell ice to an Eskimo."* It made me laugh, but it also reminded me that leadership is about persuasion, encouragement, and painting a vision so clearly that people want to be part of it.

> **GTTM** is about finding ways, big or small, to spark belief in people who don't yet see their own potential.

Leadership Principle: GTTM — Give Them the Motivation

- **Set the Challenge**: Paint a bold vision. Make it clear what success looks like.

- **Add the Incentive**: Create a fun or meaningful reward (yes, even kissing a pig).

- **Follow Through**: Keep your word. Celebrate publicly when goals are reached.

- **Make It Memorable**: Let the story live on as motivation for the next challenge.

Motivation turns effort into excellence. Give people a reason to believe, and they'll give you results you never imagined.

Building a Professional Learning Community

At Great Falls Elementary, we began building our Professional Learning Community (PLC) with a simple but powerful goal: student success. Year after year, that vision shaped our culture. Teachers met regularly to share data, develop strategies, and create common assessments. Improvement was never accidental—it was the product of reflection, collaboration, and dedication.

The PLC became the heartbeat of our school. It was under that model that we learned the importance of shared leadership, accountability, and a relentless pursuit of excellence. Teachers didn't just own their classrooms—they owned the success of every child in the building.

Family, Community, and WTO Leadership

We knew that student success couldn't be achieved in isolation. Families had to be part of the journey. That's why we created opportunities for parents to be deeply involved:

- **Parent Coffees** to share school data and goals.

- **A-TEAM Mentoring Program**, where male role models invested weekly in students struggling academically or behaviorally.

- **Monthly Parent Workshops** to build technology skills and empower families to support learning at home.

But not every parent was quick to support me when I became principal. In fact, one parent told me straight up that she didn't like me. She said I had turned the school into a prison and that I acted like I was still running a middle school. Those words cut deep—but they also forced me to make a decision.

Would I defend myself and create an enemy, or would I choose a different path?

That's when I adopted what I now call **WTO Leadership: Win Them Over.** WTO isn't about compromise—it's about connection. It's the belief that critics don't have to remain critics. Sometimes the strongest "no" can become the most passionate "yes" if you're willing to listen, respect, and invite them in.

I started calling that parent, asking for her input, and involving her in some of my decision-making processes. Before long, she joined the School Improvement Council (SIC). Soon after, she was handing out flyers, knocking on doors, and recruiting parents to join the PTO and SIC. The same parent who once resisted me became one of my biggest cheerleaders.

That experience taught me that leadership isn't about winning arguments, it's about winning hearts. WTO Leadership became a principle I carried with me: never push away a critic when you might be able to win them over.

<table><tr><td>

Leadership Principle: WTO — Win Them Over

- **Listen**: Hear concerns without defensiveness.

- **Value**: Affirm the person's perspective, even if you disagree.

- **Invite**: Bring them into the process and give them ownership.

- **Empower**: Provide opportunities for meaningful contribution.

- **Celebrate**: Acknowledge their growth and partnership publicly.

</td></tr></table>

Critics don't have to remain critics. Sometimes the loudest "no" can become your strongest "yes."

Community Events That Unite

One of our most powerful community events was the **State of Our School Symposium.** Over 150 parents and community leaders gathered for an evening of student performances, a guest speaker, and a data presentation. It wasn't just a school meeting—it was a celebration of shared purpose.

Events like this reminded us that schools don't just belong to students or staff—they belong to the community. And when the community feels ownership, students thrive.

Using Data to Drive Growth

At Great Falls, we didn't just collect data—we used it. Weekly **Data Team Meetings** brought together administrators, teachers, and coaches to analyze results and chart next steps. Pre-tests, benchmarks, running records, and post-tests provided a roadmap for intervention, enrichment, and mastery learning.

Even our students were part of the process. They met in the Data Room to discuss grade-level goals and reflect on their own progress. Data was not about numbers—it was about growth, accountability, and giving students ownership of their future.

The Global Classroom

God even expanded my influence beyond South Carolina. Through my work with Microsoft and NCCE (Northwest Council for Computer Education), I traveled the world—Prague, Spain, Amsterdam, India—training educators, inspiring students, and encouraging leaders.

Everywhere I went, I carried the same message: *"Every child can learn. Every child must learn. And every child can compete with students from around the world."*

Education became my mission field. The Great Commission doesn't stop at church doors—it extends to classrooms, conference halls, and computer labs.

Lessons from Education

Here's what I've learned from my years as an educator:

- **The classroom is a pulpit.** Every teacher preaches something— make sure it's life, not death.

- **Leadership is service.** People don't follow titles—they follow love.

- **Excellence is contagious.** When you believe in people, they rise to meet your expectations.

- **Education is global.** We are preparing students not just for today, but for the world.

- **Community matters.** Schools thrive when families, mentors, and leaders work together.

- **Practice WTO Leadership.** Critics don't have to remain critics. Sometimes the loudest "no" can become your strongest "yes."

- **Apply GTTM.** Motivation turns effort into excellence. Give people a reason to believe, and they'll give you results you never imagined.

Key Scripture
"Train up a child in the way he should go; even when he is old he will not depart from it."
— Proverbs 22:6

EDUCATOR AT HEART: REFLECTION & ACTION

1. Who in your life served as an "educator" beyond academics, teaching you life lessons you still carry?

2. How can you see your workplace as a pulpit—an opportunity to minister where you are?

3. What does servant leadership look like in your context?

4. In what ways can you engage families and communities in the mission of your work?

5. Who might God be calling you to **WTO—Win Them Over** in your own journey?

6. Where could you apply **GTTM—Give Them the Motivation** to spark belief in someone around you?

<hr>

CLOSING PRAYER

Lord, thank You for the gift of teaching and leading. Help me to see every space as a pulpit, every person as a student, and every day as an opportunity to plant seeds of hope. Make me a servant leader who values people more than position. Teach me to practice WTO Leadership, to win people over with patience, humility, and love. And teach me to apply GTTM, giving people the motivation they need to see the best in themselves. May my work always build bridges—between teachers and students, schools and families, communities and the world. Amen.

CHAPTER 10

A GLOBAL VOICE

When I first started preaching to cats and dogs on Nana's porch, I never imagined God would one day send me across the world. But that's how He works—He takes our small beginnings and multiplies them beyond what we could ever ask or think.

Education opened doors for me that I didn't even know existed. It became not just a career, but a platform—one God used to make my voice global.

From Hopkins to the World

Growing up on the dirt roads of Hopkins, South Carolina, the world felt small. My days were filled with church services, family gatherings, and community life. But God always had a bigger vision.

Through my work in education—and partnerships with Microsoft and NCCE (Northwest Council for Computer Education)—I found myself boarding planes to countries I had only read about. Prague. Spain. Amsterdam. India.

Each trip was humbling. I went from porches and pulpits to classrooms and conferences filled with educators, students, and leaders from around the world. And each time, I carried the same message:

"Every child can learn. Every child must learn. Every child deserves a chance to compete globally."

The Global Classroom

In **Prague**, I stood in rooms filled with teachers eager to learn how technology could transform their classrooms.

In **Spain**, I watched students light up as they discovered new tools that made learning exciting and interactive.

In **Amsterdam**, I spoke with leaders who weren't just concerned with test scores, but with building schools that inspired—not just instructed.

And in **India**, I walked into spaces where resources were scarce but passion was abundant. Watching students who had so little achieve so much reminded me that excellence isn't about what you have—it's about what you do with what you've got.

Everywhere I went, I realized the classroom is global. The challenges may look different, but the heart is the same: students who need encouragement, teachers who need support, and communities that need hope.

Amsterdam and Marlou van Beek

One of the most memorable invitations I ever received came from **Marlou van Beek**, a dynamic and visionary leader in the Netherlands. Marlou is the Founder and CEO of Turning Learning, a Microsoft Partner, and a cluster leader in the *New Pedagogies for Deep Learning* global partnership that connects more than 1,000 schools worldwide to accelerate learning.

Marlou once told me that she was deeply inspired by my story and by a simple phrase I often shared: *"Nothing is impossible."* To her, those words weren't just encouragement; they were a declaration that aligned with her mission of helping schools embrace deep learning, innovation, and collaboration. She saw in Great Falls Elementary a living testimony of that belief.

In 2015, she reached out with an invitation that humbled me to my core:

"Wendell is a very inspiring leader and is focused on the future of his children in his schools! Amazing how skilled Wendell is!!! I am very inspired by your story and your quote; saying nothing is impossible. This fits perfect to my profile! We have just started in a Dutch network bringing schools together, and when we talk about nothing is impossible, I would like to ask you kindly if you can give a keynote in Amsterdam."

Stepping Into the Room

When I arrived in Amsterdam, I walked into the hall where I would be speaking. Rows of chairs stood neatly arranged, waiting to be filled. Globe lights hung overhead, casting a soft glow on the room. A podium stood ready on the stage, beside a towering screen.

I paused for a moment to take it all in. I even snapped a photo of the empty room before the crowd arrived. That still image captured what my heart was feeling: awe.

I thought about Grandma's porch. I thought about the dirt roads of Hopkins, South Carolina. I thought about the students back at Great Falls who had pushed through doubt and risen to success. And now, here I was, oceans away, about to tell their story on a stage in Europe.

It felt like God whispering, *"See what I can do with your yes."*

Sharing the Story of Great Falls

When the hall filled and the chatter subsided, I stepped up to the podium. Behind me, the slide lit up with the words:

"You get what you expect. Expect the impossible, and you will be sure to receive it."

Those words set the tone.

I spoke about **Great Falls Elementary**, a school once written off as "at risk." I told them how we shifted the culture by embracing the **Professional Learning Community (PLC) model.** How teachers stopped working in silos and began collaborating around three questions:

1. What do we expect students to learn?

2. How will we know if they have learned it?

3. How will we respond if they don't — or if they already have?

I described the energy of our monthly data meetings, the courage it took to face hard truths, and the commitment of teachers who refused to let any child slip through the cracks. I shared about "Technology Tuesdays," common assessments, vertical planning, and the relentless belief that together we could move the needle.

And I told them the results: how Great Falls went from near restructuring to becoming a **South Carolina Title I Distinguished School** and eventually a **National Title I Distinguished School.**

The room grew quiet as I reminded them:

"Excellence isn't about what you have. It's about what you do with what you've got. And every child deserves our best."

The Response

When I finished, the audience leaned in even closer. Educators asked:

- *"How did you win over teachers who were tired of change?"*

- *"What kept you going when progress felt slow?"*

- *"How did you bring parents and the community along?"*

Their questions weren't just technical — they were heartfelt. They saw in our story a mirror of their own struggles. And they wanted hope.

I answered honestly, telling them about resistance, about the importance of patience, and about winning people over through persistence and servant leadership. I even shared the story of a parent who once accused me of turning the school into a "prison" — but who, through being included and empowered, became one of our biggest cheerleaders.

By the end, Marlou told me that Great Falls had become more than a case study; it was a symbol. Our journey was proof that schools facing poverty, limited resources, or doubt could still rise to excellence.

What It Meant to Me

As the room emptied and I looked back at the rows of chairs, I felt tears press against my eyes. I had stood in a historic hall in Amsterdam, but I wasn't standing there alone. I carried Hopkins with me. I carried Grandma's porch with me. I carried my students, my teachers, my family, my God.

That day, I understood more deeply than ever that my story wasn't mine alone. It was a vessel. A reminder to the world that with faith, collaboration, and persistence, *nothing is impossible.*

Salt and Light

As much as these trips were about education, they were also about ministry. I didn't always carry a Bible or stand in a pulpit, but I carried the Word in my heart. I prayed before every presentation. I spoke encouragement into every teacher I trained. I treated every student with dignity and value.

Jesus said we are the salt of the earth and the light of the world. That means ministry isn't confined to church walls—it's wherever you set your feet.

For me, that meant hotel conference rooms in Europe, classrooms in India, and auditoriums in America.

I discovered that **ministry happens when you carry Christ into your calling.**

The Weight of Responsibility

Being given a global voice was an honor, but it was also a responsibility. I didn't just represent myself. I represented my community, my family, my church, my students, and ultimately my God.

I wanted people to see that a boy from Hopkins, South Carolina, could stand shoulder to shoulder with leaders from across the world—not because of who I am, but because of who God is.

With every trip, I felt the weight of stewardship. This wasn't about me gaining stamps on a passport. It was about breaking barriers, opening doors, and showing what's possible when God orders your steps.

Lessons from a Global Voice

Traveling the world taught me:

- **The world is bigger than your block.** Don't limit yourself to where you started—God can take you places you never imagined.

- **Education is universal.** Every child everywhere deserves the chance to learn and dream.

- **Ministry is portable.** You don't need a pulpit to preach—you just need to carry Christ into your calling.

- **Representation matters.** When you step into spaces where others like you haven't been, you open the door for the next generation.

- **"Nothing is impossible" is more than a phrase.** It becomes a testimony when people see it lived out—when students who are told they can't, do; when teachers who are skeptical, lead; when communities that feel unseen, shine.

Key Scripture

"Go therefore and make disciples of all nations, baptizing them in the name of the Father and of the Son and of the Holy Spirit."
— Matthew 28:19

A GLOBAL VOICE: REFLECTION & ACTION

1. What doors has God opened in your life that felt bigger than you? How did you handle the responsibility?

2. Where can you be salt and light outside of traditional ministry spaces?

3. Who might be watching your journey and gaining courage because you stepped out in faith?

4. What "nothing is impossible" moment is God calling you to step into right now?

5. How can your story of struggle and success serve as inspiration in places far beyond where you live?

CLOSING PRAYER

Lord, thank You for expanding our reach beyond what we could imagine. Help us to see that every opportunity is an assignment, every platform is a pulpit, and every journey is a chance to represent You. Give us wisdom to carry the weight of responsibility well, courage to step into global spaces with faith and humility, and grace to let our stories encourage others to believe that they too can dream big, work hard, and see transformation come. Amen.

CHAPTER 11

FAMILY FIRST

Ministry has taken me many places. Education has opened doors I never dreamed possible. I've stood on stages, in classrooms, in pulpits, and in conference halls around the world. But at the end of the day, none of those titles matter as much as one: **Father.**

All the accolades, recognitions, and invitations mean nothing if I fail at home. This truth did not come easy to me—it was forged through tears, hard lessons, and a deep conviction that God doesn't just measure success by what you accomplish in the world, but by how you love your family.

The Gift of My Daughter

One of the greatest blessings God ever gave me was my daughter, **Kristin Marleyna.** From the moment she was born, my world changed. Her smile, her laughter, her innocence—it was like God handed me a living, breathing reminder of His love.

I still remember holding her as a baby, looking into her tiny face and thinking, *"Lord, how could You trust me with something this precious?"* In that moment, I knew that whatever else I became in life, being her father was my most sacred calling.

As she grew, Kristin became my joy and my challenge. She was strong-willed, intelligent, and full of personality. She was also perceptive. She could tell when my mind was somewhere else, when the demands of church or school pulled my focus away from her. And sometimes she let me know exactly how she felt about it.

There were moments when Kristin looked at me with hurt in her eyes and said words no father ever wants to hear: *"Daddy, I think you love the church more than you love me."*

Those words cut deeper than any criticism I've ever faced in ministry. Because while it wasn't true, from her perspective, it felt that way. And in some ways, I had given her reason to believe it.

The Struggle of Balance

You see, my daughter lived with her mother, not with me. That reality added an extra layer of difficulty to fatherhood. Distance is hard for any parent, but when you combine that with the unrelenting demands of ministry and education, the weight becomes even heavier.

I was there for other people's children—for their ball games, their graduations, their crises. I was the pastor who showed up. I was the principal who gave his all. But sometimes my daughter felt left behind in the shadow of my service.

That's the tension every leader faces: the pull between public responsibility and private responsibility. The church needed me. The school needed me. But my daughter needed me, too. And no matter how noble the cause, neglect at home leaves a wound that titles can't heal.

I didn't always get it right. In fact, I got it wrong more times than I care to admit. But in those failures, God taught me a critical lesson: **Your first ministry is your family.**

Ministry Begins at Home

Scripture makes it clear: *"If anyone does not know how to manage his own family, how can he take care of God's church?"* (1 Timothy 3:5). The truth is, leadership in any form—whether spiritual, educational, or professional—loses credibility if it doesn't start with faithfulness at home.

Being a father isn't just a biological fact; it's a calling. Just as a church needs a pastor and a school needs a principal, a child needs a father. And if I failed at that, everything else I accomplished would ring hollow.

So I began to shift. I became more intentional about showing up—not just physically, but emotionally. I carved out time to call, to listen, to create moments that belonged only to her. Even if we weren't under the same roof, I wanted her to know that no matter how many people called me "Pastor" or "Principal," she could always call me "Dad."

Work-Life Balance: Lessons Learned

Balancing ministry, leadership, and family is one of the hardest struggles any leader will ever face. Here are some lessons I learned the hard way:

1. **You have to say "no" to good things to say "yes" to the best things.**
   There will always be another meeting, another crisis, another demand. But your child will only be seven once. Only have their first recital once. Only graduate once.

2. **Presence is greater than proximity.**
   Living in the same house doesn't automatically mean you're present. Presence is about attention, not just geography.

3. **Protect the calendar.**
   If you don't schedule time for your family, others will schedule it for you. Treat family time like you treat board meetings or Sunday services—non-negotiable.

4. **Rest is not selfish—it's stewardship.**
   Ministry and education can consume every ounce of energy if you let them. But burnout helps no one. Sabbath rest is a command, not a suggestion.

5. **Invite your family into your world.**

   Sometimes balance doesn't mean separation—it means integration. Let your children see what you do. Let them participate in your calling when appropriate, so they feel part of it, not pushed aside by it.

The Gift of My Granddaughter

Years later, God gave me another blessing I never saw coming: my granddaughter, **Mariah Trinity**.

I remember the day she was born as if it were yesterday. The moment I laid eyes on her, I cried. At first, I asked myself, *"Why am I crying? She's my granddaughter, not my child."* But then I understood.

Mariah is deeply connected to me—not just biologically, but spiritually. God placed a special bond between us that I can't even fully explain. She is tender, wise beyond her years, and full of joy.

At just seven years old, Mariah already serves in my church. She loves the Lord, loves her PaPa, and walks with a wisdom far beyond her age. I'll never forget my 32nd Church Anniversary. In the middle of all the celebration, she sat beside me, looked up with her big eyes, and said words that shook me to my core:

"Papa, I will never leave you."

In that moment, it was as if God Himself was reminding me of His eternal promise through the words of my granddaughter. That's legacy. That's ministry.

Joy in the Journey

I don't want you to think my family's story is only about struggle. There's been so much laughter, too. Kristin and I shared countless moments of joy—from her first dance recital to road trips filled with off-key singing and inside jokes.

Mariah brings me the kind of laughter only a grandchild can bring—the kind where you forget the weight of the world and just delight in the innocence of a child's smile.

These moments matter. They remind me that balance isn't just about managing tension; it's about savoring joy.

Practical Strategies for Balance

If you're a leader trying to juggle multiple responsibilities, here are some strategies that helped me:

- **Establish Family Rituals**: Weekly dinners, bedtime calls, or Saturday morning breakfasts create anchors of connection.

- **Use Technology Wisely**: A text, a video call, or a voice note can remind your child you're thinking of them—even from miles away.

- **Set Boundaries**: Learn to say, *"I can't do that right now, I have family commitments."* People will respect you more when they see you respect your family.

- **Practice WTO and GTTM at Home**: Win Them Over by listening and involving your family. Give Them the Motivation by celebrating even small milestones.

- **Model Balance for Others**: Your staff, congregation, and colleagues are watching. Show them what it means to lead without losing your family.

A Different Kind of Legacy

When I think about legacy, I don't just think about sermons I've preached or schools I've led. I think about Kristin and Mariah. I think about the lessons they've learned from watching me—the good and the not-so-good. I think about the ways they'll carry forward faith, resilience, and love.

Because at the end of the day, the truest measure of my ministry is not how many members filled the pews or how many students filled the classrooms—it's how well I loved my family, and how deeply they knew they were loved.

Lessons from Fatherhood

Here's what I've learned:

- **Your family is your first church.** Love them, lead them, and cover them in prayer.

- **Presence matters more than proximity.** Even if you don't live under the same roof, your child still needs to feel your love.

- **Balance takes intentionality.** You can't just hope it happens—you have to plan for it.

- **Legacy begins at home.** The world may forget your titles, but your children will never forget your love.

- **Work-life balance is spiritual discipline.** When you honor your family, you honor God.

Key Scripture

"But if anyone does not provide for his relatives, and especially for members of his household, he has denied the faith and is worse than an unbeliever."
— 1 Timothy 5:8

FAMILY FIRST: REFLECTION & ACTION

1. In what ways do you sometimes give more to others than to your own family?

2. How can you be more intentional about showing your loved ones that they are your first priority?

3. What boundaries could you set this week to protect family time?

4. What legacy do you want your children and grandchildren to re-member about you?

5. How can you integrate WTO and GTTM into your family relationships?

───────── CLOSING PRAYER ─────────

Lord, thank You for the gift of family. Teach me to balance my responsibilities with wisdom and grace. Help me to be intentional with my time, present with my heart, and faithful in my love. Remind me that my first ministry is not in the pulpit or the classroom, but in my home. May my legacy be one of love, faith, and presence. Amen.

CHAPTER 12

BLESSED TO BE A BLESSING

As I look back over my life, I can say with confidence: I am blessed. Not because it has been easy. Not because I never struggled. Not because everything went the way I planned. But because through it all, God has been faithful.

From the dirt roads of Hopkins to the pulpit of Zion Mill Creek…
From a boy who was told he wasn't "college material" to an educator shaping schools and students…
From preaching to cats and dogs on Nana's porch to preaching across nations…
From crying at my mother's bedside to crying tears of joy at my granddaughter's words…

Every season has been covered by God's hand. And as I reflect, I realize that every blessing I have received has not been for me alone. God blessed me to be a blessing.

The Blessing of Struggle

Struggles don't feel like blessings in the moment. They hurt. They drain you. They leave you questioning. But as I look back, I see how every struggle became a stepping stone.

Being placed in the wrong class in high school lit a fire in me. I could have accepted what they said about me—that I wasn't "college material." Instead, I chose to prove them wrong. That moment of misplacement forced me to discover resilience I didn't know I had.

When I got to college, I carried that determination with me. Every time I felt like quitting, I remembered the voices that had doubted me. And I reminded myself that their words didn't define me. God did. That struggle became my drive, shaping the educator I would one day become.

Losing my mother to cancer was another storm that nearly broke me. I can still remember sitting by her bedside, watching the strongest woman I had ever known grow weaker day by day. I prayed, I pleaded, I wept. And when God didn't answer the way I wanted Him to, I had to decide whether I would walk away in bitterness or lean into His arms. I chose to lean. And in that season of grief, I discovered a depth of God's comfort I had never known before.

Even my struggle to balance fatherhood with ministry and leadership became a blessing in disguise. It forced me to face the reality that success in public means little if you fail at home. It taught me that love is not just something you preach—it's something you show in intentional, consistent ways.

Struggles are like rain. Nobody enjoys being caught in a storm. The sky darkens, the winds whip, and the downpour soaks you to the bone. But once the storm passes, the flowers bloom, the rivers flow stronger, and seeds that were buried deep begin to grow. That's how God uses struggles. They water the soil of our souls, and over time, what looked like loss produces fruit.

The struggles didn't break me—they built me. And for that, I am blessed.

The Blessing of People

No one arrives where I am by themselves. If my life is blessed, it is because God surrounded me with people who poured into me.

First, there was **Nana**. Her life was my first sermon. She prayed with a power that made heaven pay attention. She shouted with such joy that the whole neighborhood knew we belonged to God. She didn't just tell me about faith—she showed me what it looked like lived out loud.

Then there was my grandmother, **Julia Dowdy**. If Nana was the fire, Julia was the calm. Her porch was my first pulpit. Her home was a place of refuge. After church, after school, after storms of life, we found peace in her presence. She didn't raise her voice often, but when she spoke, her words carried weight. She was proof that strength doesn't always shout—sometimes it whispers.

God also gave me **mentors** who corrected me when I was off track, church mothers who hugged me when I felt invisible, and colleagues who sharpened me. Some of those colleagues stretched me in ways I didn't enjoy at the time. They challenged my ideas, questioned my methods, and pushed me to grow. Looking back, I see that even their friction was a blessing. Iron sharpens iron.

And then, of course, my family. My siblings who walked with me through grief and laughter. My daughter Kristin, who made me a father. My granddaughter, Mariah, who made me "PaPa," reminded me that blessings multiply across generations.

Every blessing in my life bears the fingerprints of other people. And I am grateful.

The Blessing of Ministry

When I first became pastor at Zion Mill Creek, the church was small. The sanctuary wasn't much to look at, and the floorboards carried more history than polish. On Sundays, when the saints got to shouting, the floor would literally bounce beneath our feet. You could feel the whole building moving as if heaven itself was stomping along with us.

I'll never forget one Sunday when the choir sang one of those old songs that everybody knew. The tambourine clapped, the deacons swayed, and before long the Spirit had swept through the sanctuary.

The floor bounced so hard I thought we might crash straight into the basement. But nobody cared. The Spirit had filled the house, and we were lost in worship.

Some would have called it a weakness. I called it a testimony. That bouncing floor reminded me of Acts 16, when Paul and Silas prayed and sang hymns in prison, and the earth shook. We didn't need marble floors or stained-glass windows. All we needed was a place to gather, hearts ready to praise, and a God big enough to fill the room.

Years later, when we built our new sanctuary, I marveled at what God had done. From bouncing floorboards to a strong, beautiful building, the journey wasn't about wood and nails—it was about faith. The new church is a blessing, but I'll never forget the old one. Every time I step into our sanctuary today, I carry with me the sound of those creaking boards and the memory of a little church that shook with worship.

Zion Mill Creek isn't just a church; it's a family. Together we've laughed, cried, prayed, and praised. We've shouted through storms and celebrated victories. We've learned that even when the pews are empty, God still fills the house. Ministry has not always been easy, but it has always been worth it.

The Blessing of Education

Education was never separate from my calling—it was an extension of it.

I was once the student who doubted himself. I was once the boy placed in the wrong class, told I wasn't college material. That pain became the fuel for my passion. Because I knew what it felt like to be underestimated, I made it my mission to never let a child sit in my classroom or walk through my office without hearing: *"You matter. You can succeed. You are capable."*

At Great Falls Elementary, I saw what was possible when teachers believed in every student. Building a Professional Learning Community wasn't just about raising test scores—it was about raising expectations. Teachers no longer saw themselves as isolated in their classrooms. They became part of a team, responsible for every child in the building. And under that model, we didn't just meet goals—we surpassed them.

God opened doors for me I never dreamed possible. Microsoft and NCCE took me from Hopkins to Prague, Spain, Amsterdam, and India. In each place, I told the story of a small-town school in South Carolina that refused to settle for less. And everywhere I went, I saw the same truth: education is global. Every child everywhere deserves the chance to learn.

The classroom was my pulpit. The students were my congregation. And every lesson was a sermon of hope.

Blessed to Be a Blessing

When I count my blessings, I realize they were never meant for me alone.

God blessed me with faith so I could strengthen others.
He blessed me with opportunities so I could open doors for others.
He blessed me with love so I could pour love into others.

Every blessing I've received has come with a responsibility: to give it away.

That's why I developed principles like **WTO (Win Them Over)** and **GTTM (Give Them the Motivation)**. WTO reminds me that even critics can become cheerleaders if you serve them with humility and respect. GTTM reminds me that motivation matters—that sometimes the silly act of kissing a pig can inspire students to believe in themselves. These aren't just leadership strategies—they're ways of multiplying blessings.

Blessings are not meant to be hoarded. They are meant to flow through us to others.

How to Turn Blessings Into Blessings for Others

1. **Share Your Story.** Your testimony might be the encouragement someone else needs.

2. **Mentor Someone.** Invest in a younger leader, a student, or a child who needs direction.

3. **Serve Faithfully.** Use your gifts not for recognition, but for impact.

4. **Celebrate Others.** Blessings multiply when you create joy for others.

5. **Stay Humble.** Never forget that everything you have comes from God's hand.

A Legacy of Gratitude

When I think about legacy, I don't just think about sermons I've preached or schools I've led. I think about Kristin and Mariah. I think about my students, my church members, my colleagues, and the countless people I've met along the way.

Legacy is not built in titles or buildings—it's built in people. The greatest testimony of my life will not be my name on a program or a plaque, but the lives touched, the faith passed on, and the blessings multiplied.

I started on dirt roads. I preached to cats and dogs. I worshiped in a sanctuary where the floor bounced. But look what the Lord has done. I am blessed—and I am blessed to be a blessing.

Key Scripture
"The LORD bless you and keep you; the LORD make his face shine on you and be gracious to you; the LORD turn his face toward you and give you peace."
— Numbers 6:24–26

BLESSED TO BE A BLESSING: REFLECTION & ACTION

1. When you look back over your life, what blessings stand out most clearly?

2. Who has been a blessing in your journey that you need to thank God for?

3. How is God calling you to use your blessings to bless others?

4. In what ways can you practice WTO or GTTM to multiply blessings?

5. What legacy of blessing do you want to leave behind?

CLOSING PRAYER

Lord, thank You for every blessing You've poured into my life—seen and unseen. Thank You for carrying me through struggles, surrounding me with people, calling me into ministry, and opening doors I never imagined. Help me to use every blessing not for my glory, but for Yours. And may my life be a testimony that You are faithful. Amen.

ABOUT THE AUTHOR

Wendell B. Sumter

Pastor | Educator | Leader | Motivational Speaker

Wendell B. Sumter hails from Columbia, SC, and was born on February 9, 1968. He is the proud son of the late Mrs. Luella S. Dinkins and Mr. Herbert Neal, and the stepson of Mr. Willie Dinkins, Sr., the grandson of the late Rubin and Juliette Neal and Julia Dowdy and Joseph Sumter, and the oldest of five siblings. Wendell is a devoted father to his daughter, Kristin Marleyna Sumter, and a proud grandfather to Mariah Trinity Williams.

Growing up in the close-knit community of Hopkins, SC, Wendell was shaped by humble beginnings and a deep foundation of faith. Ordained to preach in 1990, he began ministry at Zion Benevolent Baptist Church, serving as Associate Pastor and leading youth and music ministries. Since 1993, he has faithfully pastored Zion Mill Creek Baptist Church in Columbia, SC, where he has overseen remarkable growth in membership, property, ministries, and spiritual rededications.

In addition to ministry, Wendell has devoted over 30 years to public education. He earned a Bachelor of Science in Elementary Education from Morris College and a Master's in Education from the University of South Carolina. He has taught elementary and middle school students, served as Assistant Principal at Lower Richland High School, and later became Principal of both Great Falls Middle and Great Falls Elementary. Under his leadership, these schools received national recognition, including Microsoft Showcase School status and Title I Distinguished School awards.

Currently, Wendell serves as Assistant Superintendent of Human Resources for Chester County School District, where he leads educator recruitment, retention, and development. His professional influence extends globally—he has served as a member of the Microsoft Education Advisory Board, a Learning Specialist with the Northwest Council for Computer Education (NCCE), and as a Microsoft Innovative Educator and Trainer. His work has taken him across the world to Prague, Spain, Amsterdam, and India, where he has inspired educators, leaders, and students alike.

As a pastor, motivational speaker, morale booster, and proven leader, Wendell believes that every child can learn and must be prepared to compete globally   . His life's work—in both ministry and education—embodies his belief that he is "blessed to be a blessing."

TAKE THE NEXT STEP ON YOUR JOURNEY

Invite Wendell B. Sumter to Your Next Event

Wendell B. Sumter is a sought-after speaker, pastor, and educational leader who has inspired audiences from the dirt roads of South Carolina to the global stages of Amsterdam and India.

Whether you are looking to motivate a school staff, empower a congregation, or train a corporate leadership team, Wendell brings a unique blend of humor, vulnerability, and proven strategies.

Signature Keynotes & Workshops:

- **Dirt Road Destiny:** Overcoming labels and embracing God's timing.
- **GTTM (Give Them the Motivation):** Strategies for high-impact leadership.
- **WTO (Win Them Over):** Turning critics into champions for your vision.
- **The Balanced Life Plan:** Leading with excellence without losing your family.

Book Wendell Today: www.wendellbsumter.com wendell@wendellbsumter.com @wendellbsumter

ACKNOWLEDGMENTS

No story is written alone. My life has been shaped by family, friends, mentors, educators, and church members who carried me when I could not carry myself. This book is not just my story—it is our story.

First, I thank **God**, the Author and Finisher of my faith, for blessing me to be a blessing.

To my family, who laid the foundation of love and faith:

- My grandmother, the late **Juliette D. Neal**, my father's mother—"Nana"—whose strong faith and powerful prayers showed me what it meant to truly trust God.

- My grandfather, the late **Rubin Neal**, who stood as a pillar of strength and family pride, and showed up to church every Sunday when I became a pastor.

- My father, the late **Herbert Neal**, who gave me my name and my roots.

- My mother, the late **Luella Sumter Dinkins**, whose love, resilience, and fight taught me more about strength than any book ever could.

- My stepfather, **Willie Dinkins Sr.**, who stepped into my life with guidance and care.

- My grandmother, the late **Julia Sims Dowdy**, my mother's mother, whose house was the refuge of peace, the gathering place after church, and the shelter when life's storms overwhelmed my mom. She gave us calm when we needed it most.

To my siblings:

- My sister **LaMaryann Shiver**,
- My sister **Sonjia Neal**,
- My sister **Necole Neal**,
- My brother **Willie Dinkins Jr.**

Each of you has been a part of my story, my support, and my love.

To **all of my Cousins, Aunts and Uncles**—thank you for the laughter, the encouragement, the memories, and the countless ways you reminded me that family is more than blood; it is love.

To my daughter, **Kristin Marleyna**, who made me a father and taught me the meaning of legacy. And to my granddaughter, **Mariah Trinity**, who captured my heart the moment she was born, and whose words—*"Papa, I will never leave you"*—will forever echo in my soul.

To Zakos, who has honored me with the title of 'Pops' and walked alongside me as a son of my heart. Thank you for your loyalty, your strength, and your love. You have reminded me that fatherhood is not defined solely by blood, but by the commitment we make to lead and love those God places in our care. I am proud to be your father, and I am proud of the man you are.

To my church family at **Zion Mill Creek Baptist Church**—thank you for allowing me to serve as your pastor, for walking with me through storms and victories, and for teaching me that the church is not a building but a people who love and serve God together.

To my colleagues and fellow educators—thank you for standing alongside me in classrooms, hallways, and conference rooms, proving that education is not just about academics, but about building futures.

And to every friend, mentor, mentee, former student and supporter not named here but forever etched in my heart—thank you.

This book carries all of your fingerprints. My story is stronger because you are a part of it.